EKATERINOSLAV:

ONE FAMILY'S PASSAGE
TO AMERICA

EKATERINOSLAV:

ONE FAMILY'S PASSAGE
TO AMERICA

⁓

A Memoir in Verse by
Jane Yolen

HOLY COW! PRESS :: DULUTH, MINNESOTA :: 2012

First printing, 2012

ISBN 978-09833254-6-8

10 9 8 7 6 5 4 3 2 1

Library of Congress Cataloging-in-Publication Data
Yolen, Jane.
Ekaterinoslav : one family's passage to America, a memoir in verse / by Jane Yolen.
p. cm.
ISBN 978-0-9833254-6-8 (alk. paper)
1. Yolen, Jane—Family—Poetry. 2. Authors, American—20th century—Biography. I.
Title.
PS3575.O43Z46 2012
811'.54—dc23 [B] 2012009675

This project is supported in part by grant awards from the Ben and Jeanne Overman Charitable Trust, the Elmer L. and Eleanor J. Andersen Foundation, the Cy and Paula DeCosse Fund of the Minneapolis Foundation, and by gifts from individual donors.

Holy Cow! Press books are distributed to the trade by: Consortium Book Sales & Distribution, c/o Perseus Distribution, 210 American Drive, Jackson, TN 38301.

For personal inquiries, write to: Holy Cow! Press, Post Office Box 3170, Mount Royal Station, Duluth, Minnesota 55803.

Please visit our website: www.holycowpress.org

ACKNOWLEDGMENTS

THE PALE © 2011 published, *Pirene's Fountain* 2011.

CHOLERA © 1991, published in the anthology *Colors of a New Day: Writing for South Africa*, ed. Sarah LeFanu & Stephen Hayward, Pantheon Books 1991. Published there as "Small Pox" but I've since learned better.

ROUND FRAME © 2001, published in *North American Review* as "Oval Frame" 2001.

FURS © 2006, published in *New England Watershed Magazine* 2006.

WILL © 1992, published in The *Magazine of Speculative Poetry*, Spring 1992, Vol 3, No 3, and as a broadside from A Midsummer Night's Press, Spring 1992.

ABOUT THE PHOTOGRAPHS

Page 2, "Picture This," archival photograph of a typical shtetl street. Taken at shtetl Shkudvil, Russia, circa 1910. Image courtesy of Jewishgen.org.

Page 11, "Round Frame," photograph of my father Will which he gave to me when I was in my 40's.

Page 16, "First Wave," archival photograph of the *S. S. Dwinsk* which later carried the last six members of the Yolens to America in 1914. Image courtesy of Maritime-Historical Ship Research Database (7seasvessels.com).

Page 19, "Photograph," in Ekaterinoslav, the entire family; the photograph on the table is of Lou, already gone.

Page 23, "Manifests," archival photograph of the actual manifest of the third wave of Yolens, note spelling of the name (Yolin), and my father's name Wolf. Image courtesy of Ellis Island Foundation.

Page 32, "Dapper Dan," photograph of Lou, from his family's scrapbook.

Page 37, "Middle Class," photograph of Samson and Mina Yolen after they'd been 18 years in America, probably in New Haven.

Page 38, "Bottle," one of three still in the family, this one is mine, given to me by my uncle Harry and his wife Isabelle. Photograph by Jason Stemple.

Page 43, "Cousins," or at least all of them born by 1930. Grandma and Grandpa are in the middle, with Lou's mother-in-law next to them.

Page 52, "About the Author," my mother and father, and me between them, circa 1940.

DEDICATION

For the Yolens, past and present, as well as my own family: Heidi Elisabeth Yolen Stemple, Adam Douglas Stemple, Jason Frederic Stemple and their children. *L'Chaim.*

For my Tuesday writing group who listened to these poems with patience, attention, and good solid critiques. *A mitzvah.*

For my cousins whose research into our family genealogy—threadbare and full of *bobbemysehs*—I have borrowed from all of you, but especially from Sandy Hack, Bob and Harriet Yolen, and Martin Weiss. *Dank times four.*

And with great thanks to Jim Perlman, most gracious of editors. *A broche.*

My father's family lived in Ekaterinoslav in the Ukraine, in a small Jewish village, the Yiddish term for which is *shtetl*. The family existed under the iron will of Grandma Mina (or Minna or Minnie) Hyatt Yolen, aka "The Duchess," and her dapper husband, Samson Yolen, who was by profession a bottler, by avocation a storyteller. Mina and Samson had two (or three) children who died in a cholera epidemic leaving only one—Lou—alive. After that, Mina was crazy with grief and certain G-d had punished her for something, until she gave birth to twin girls, Eva and Sylvia. Then she was convinced G-d had forgiven her. The rest of the eight living children followed quickly, though I am not certain Mina ever forgave G-d.

I didn't know that my father (as his father before him) had been born in Ekaterinoslav until I was in my mid-thirties. I didn't know my grandfather's birth date (April 1860) until I was in my seventies and saw his signed "Declaration of Intention" on entering the country. My dad had always intimated to both my brother and me that his birthplace had been New Haven, or Waterbury. The geography seemed to move around Connecticut when I wasn't looking. In fact according to the Ellis Island records, he was actually seven years old when he landed in America.

So I never had a true picture of the family compound, bordered on one side by trenches where Russian (or Ukrainian) soldiers held maneuvers. I only know that much because my Uncle Harry and some of my older cousins told me about it after my father died.

One cousin sent me information that Ekaterinoslav (or Yketerinislav) has been renamed and is now a huge city called Dnipropetrovsk, but as there was also a city in Russia proper called Ekaterinoslav, I don't know which one he means. I don't know if even *he* knows. So history surprises and disguises. The records of the shetls, devastated and made into nightmarish killing grounds by the Nazis, are terribly incomplete.

Like many of the more than two million Jews of The Pale who immigrated to America from 1880 onwards, the Yolens came over in waves. First the eldest son Lou was sent ahead, arriving in October 1912 at age 22. The following year the three oldest girls—twins Sylvia and Eva, and younger sister Vera—made the journey, finding work as milliners. In 1914, Grandma Mina, Grandpa Samson, and the four younger children came across the ocean. My father—who was called Velvul/Wolf/William/Will/Billy/Bill, take your pick—was the second youngest.

In the new country, in New Haven and Waterbury, my grandfather rebuilt his bottling business with Lou doing much of the hard work. And—so the stories go—Lou did some bootlegging as well. At one point, the family owned a Coca Cola franchise but sold it before the magic formula was added which made millionaires of others, but not us.

Alas, that family—mother, father, eight siblings—are gone now and so I have no one to check with about the facts in these poems except my cousins and second cousins who know only a bit more than I do. As the Yolens are all storytellers, making up what we don't really know or remember, I can't vouch for the authenticity of what I've been told. But the major truths (as opposed to the facts) are here. That's what poetry does best anyway—turning the dry rota of history into something beautiful and true.

Why do these poems end in 1939? That's when I was born, and a new Yolen history began. For me, Ekaterinoslav had very little to do with what came after—until now.

—Jane Yolen, 2012

TABLE OF CONTENTS

Ekaterinoslav 1873-1913

Picture this small shtetl,
packed dirt streets
rutted with market day traffic.
In the town center,
Jews sell eggs, cheese, chickens, milk.
In front of the butcher shop,
close by the blacksmith's,
my grandfather sets up a stall.
His bottles of kerosene,
like good soldiers—
upright, polished, shining—
stand in five straight lines.
A river of gentiles flows in
almost drowning the shtetl's population,
moving sluggishly amongst the Jews.
The sound of Ukrainian, Yiddish, Russian
rattles around the stalls.
The speakers talk about weather
and whether the rains will catch them out.
A gezunt ahf dein kop!
Good health on your head.
They argue about the price of flour, vodka,
grain for the cows, but never about the tsar.
That's a topic for the hidden places:
hedgerows, houses, shul.
A feier zol im trefen!
He should burn up!
Some things are best never said aloud.
For a while gentile and Jew
sound like intimates,
but no one is really fooled.
Religion, history, language, custom—
like the walls of a medieval city—
keep them divided,
their prejudices holding them
for now, for this moment, alive
and apart.

Here, in the Tsars' Pale of Settlement,
the provinces outside Russia proper,
where abruptly, arbitrarily authorities send the Jews,
we are confined, restricted, controlled.
Not a prison or ghetto or death camp
only a separate and unequal safe poverty.

Here schools are Jew schools, the learning
honey sweet on the lips of the boys,
long hours reading Hebrew, speaking Yiddish.
Theology lives in the shul next to the ark.
But philosophy—that conversation between men and G-d—
takes place on the shtetl streets,
the cobbler comparing his last
to the shaping of Adam and the rib pull of Eve,
the peddler speaking of the road to eternity,
the fishmonger praising the beauty of the carp.
This is populism of the untutored, when men,
touched by the cosmos, find their own words.

Here women clean, sew, milk the cows;
they cook, raise children, light candles, bless the table.
Yentas gossip, little knowing that gossip
is not just tittle-tattle, but the beginning of story:
our story, herstory, theirstory, history,
carried mouth to ear over and over and over again
until it becomes as true as theology, philosophy;
more true, perhaps, because we remember it
and pass it on.

COSSACKS

Turks, Tatars, Russians, Ukrainians,
what does it matter their origin
when too much vodka has been drunk
and the knife is at your throat.
Even the tsar, whom they worship,
cannot control them, saying
the Cossacks live as they please.
What pleases them, when drunk,
is to make our lives miserable.

Gogol has much to answer for.
I read *Taras Bulba* for a Russian class,
in my comfortable Smith College dorm,
dreaming of its heroes on horseback,
the "son who denies blood and country
for a woman in the enemy camp."
Bookish I, who'd never been in an enemy camp,
knew the Cossacks as lusty, proud warriors.
I dreamed of Andriy holding me in his arms.
Do we not all dream of pirates, thieves,
heroes to all excepting their victims?
Who is an easier victim than the Jew?

A hundred years removed from that knife,
I hold the blade in my hand, cutting my fingers
till they are wet with blood and ancestral tears.
"Forgive me," I whisper, to my past,
"I did not know."
"I did not understand."

First it looks like a mob,
afire with vodka or schnapps,
but soon the weapons—
knives, whips, cudgels, even guns—
tell a different tale.
The officials condone this,
looting incidental to the beatings.
Dead, we Jews are no use to them,
but beaten we are like whipped dogs
who come when they are called.
Here in old Odessa, in the Pale
pogroms are conversion by knife,
as if that gentle Jewish Christ
would have sanctioned
this brutal transubstantiation:
our Hebrew blood for their wine.

When grandpa was a young man,
all of Kiev tangled in a pogrom,
a wildfire burning across four years.
Kaddish was said in every shul,
on every street corner.
In every home the candles burned.
Dreams of America were born then
in the little houses where amulets
with the names of three angels
hung over the cradles of newborns
to keep the babies safe from demons
and from their Ukrainian cousins
who came in the night,
not with vodka,
but with cudgels and knives.

At seventeen, half-orphaned, outspoken,
literate and numerate, keeper of her father's books,
she could pass as a Ukranian peasant,
driving horse and cart ahead of the Cossacks
to rescue Jews and hide them in cellars.
She was considered unmarriageable by the aunts.
They honked about her single state,
called her father selfish, brought in a *shadchan*,
a matchmaker, to find her a suitable mate.
But like a peasant's mule, she balked
at any arrangement they tried to make,
till she heard about a young man, who spoke
many languages more than Yiddish,
visiting his brother and helping with his work.
Without permission, she dressed in black,
veiled, disguised, accompanied by the maid,
went off to the store to get a look
like some princess out of a tale,
came home and made the match herself.
Scandalized, the aunts, shook
their fingers at her, but her papa
knew she would be happy and make
many babies, and the girls would all take
after her, smart and funny and quick.

My grandmother lay down
in her Ukrainian bed,
two children at her breast,
one child at her back,
and one curled, doglike, at her feet,
all touched by fire
and the calculus of pain.
They lay in their sweat
like herrings in brine.
Ekaterinoslav,
Ekaterinoslav,
who mourns the children,
who calculates their loss,
the village so halved
it was beyond weeping.
She lay down with four,
arose with one.
How could she get up,
now knowing God's casual mathematics,
the subtraction that so divided
her uncountable heart.

Names

Louis, the scamp,
from the first family.
The twins Eva and Sylvia,
an inch and a pound apart
from the start.
Vera, sweet as summer fruit.
Sam, ill-fitted linchpin.
Rose the pocket Venus,
Will the self-proclaimed outlier.
Harry the baby.
Not their real names, of course,
only what they were given at Ellis Island,
little markers like Hansel's white stones
flung into the witch's forest
that they might find their way forward,
not back, through the New World woods.

My father's past lies hidden in a round frame.
The child there has plump cheeks,
uncolored eyes; a heavy Russian hat
perches awkwardly on his baby curls.
He stares out at me, through me, daring me
to take away his manufactured birth
in Connecticut. All those years Ekaterinoslav
was lost to me, when I could have celebrated
Ukrainian winters, learned words of love,
fashion, passion, paternity;
how to season the fish with pepper, not sugar;
how to cut the farfl from flat sheets of dough.
All I had was New Haven.
Would I go there now, when Ekaterinoslav
no longer exists; go and see
what Cossacks, Hitler, Chernobyl could not conquer,
the little shtetl my father alone destroyed
by never speaking its name?
No, I shall stay here, at home, instead,
gazing back at the boy who stares at me,
whisper to him, through him, dare him,
"Tell me the story of Ekaterinoslav,"
till one day the picture itself speaks.

With her red hair, blue eyes,
my grandmother did not look Jewish,
though Irish and Scots were in short supply
in the shtetls of the Ukraine.
My husband suggests some great-great
many-times-great grandmother
back in the tenth century
surprised by a handsome Viking,
the Swedes running an empire in nearby Kiev.
I try to think of the Hyatts, my grandmother's people,
being blowbacks, bar sinister folk,
rolling around in a cart with a blonde giant,
or in the back room of a country inn
with a lusty nobody named Sven.
My imagination stutters, fails.
Besides an iron fist and an infectious laugh—
or perhaps because of them—
Grandma Mina was the very definition
of a Jewish merchant's wife.

"The sons of God saw the daughters of men that they [were] fair. . ."
—Genesis 6:2

Behind the family house, in mock trenches,
Russian soldiers practice war.
Surely they notice the pretty Jewish girls,
on their way to market, planting seeds,
hanging laundry, dark heads together,
laughing at the gawking men behind them.
Does Eva glance back with an encouraging smile?
Does Vera trade winks with the handsome sergeant?
Does Sylvia dream of lying down in the furrows,
a general's hand on her breast, between her thighs?
I'm certain the Duchess, keeps her switch to hand.
Her daughters have suitors waiting in America,
maybe a doctor, lawyer, a rich Jewish merchant.
Maybe a dentist, a butcher, a man with a mercantile shop.
Grandma is ready to battle any soldier foolish enough
to whistle at her beautiful daughters,
wingless on the roads of earth.

PASSAGE: 1910-1914

We do not know how easily he leaves,
escaping his father's wrath,
his mother's tears,
his sisters' casual relief,
the younger children's disbelief.
Does he turn and smile? Blow kisses?
Does he use the front of his hand, the back,
as if leaving takes no courage at all?
Or is he already far-seeing,
like a sailor well used to travel,
eyes squinting into the sun;
imagining the road to the big ship,
plotting the route across the waves,
dreaming of America's streets
shining in the sun like gold.
Surely, he'd already counted
the cards to be played,
having learned in his old school
to gamble the Russian way:
no mercy given, none received.

The oldest son, Lou—the rascal, the scamp—
who gambled away the gold buttons
on his school uniform and was sent home,
is sent on even further, to America,
the family's gamble, that he will make something
of himself.

       For the family, a wager of time,
of hope, that one commodity they have in common
with other travelers.

       Lou does what is demanded,
sailing from Hamburg on a pearly September morning,
eyeing the horizon, a careful line drawn
under his future.

       In America he needs to curb a nature
that lurches towards the unruly, for at least as long
as it takes to bring three sisters, then the rest of the family
to his adopted shore.

       Seven years he works like Jacob
who labored for a wedding he didn't really want,
till Papa becomes a citizen, taking back the family reins
so Lou might grab the ring, the family jewels,
gambling again, this time his entire life
on the lawless streets of New Haven.

PHOTOGRAPH: A PROSE POEM

Wide-eyed, like a herd of deer in the wild, the family stares
out, as if flight is anticipated, desired, inevitable. Caught
in that moment, they expect a flash of light, the sound of a
shot. The wait seems unbearable, forever. Only my father, a
young buck in the making, challenges the view-finder. His
brothers, sisters, parents calculate the path, do the math,
map the escape route, contemplate the rough run ahead.

The eldest, Lou, no longer has a place here, except in a small
photograph, world within world. He stands on the table, framed
in formal black and white, like an ancestor no one remembers,
no one cares to remember. But at summer's end, his mother
touches the picture with a handkerchief. Lou is all that is left
from her first family, dead of cholera. Now an ocean is between
them, the boats too small, the miles too many, the fears too great
for anything but prayers to a G-d she no longer entirely trusts.

First Oranges

It is a sharp, sweet taste, like freedom, Vera thinks,
the color like the gold in the streets,
though they are still an ocean away from America
and she has only heard of those golden cobbles.
Rotterdam is the door into a future and she means
to devour it as she does the orange, keeping one for herself.
The paving beneath her feet, the high-stepping horses,
the gabble of the stolid Dutchmen and their wives,
the fat soprano at the opera with a voice like liquid silver,
she sucks on the memories as she sucked on the orange pips,
reluctant even years later, to let the sharp, sweet memory go.

SECOND WAVE: THE GIRLS HOLD HANDS ACROSS THE SEA

They have never seen such dark water,
endless, like the mind of G-d.
The boat plunges through troughs,
shaking with the force of them,
and Vera weeps, afraid.
But the twins cry out with a wild joy
they never show when on land,
hands clasped so tightly, their fingers whiten,
as if they are still wombed, bonded,
though ashore they hardly ever touch.

Ahead, behind, porpoises shadow the ship,
guardians from a different culture,
riding in-between the keel's shadows.
The girls give themselves to the pagan,
even Vera, who in that instant of recognition,
thinks, "This is what becoming new means,
what becoming an American is about."
Afterwards, she spends as much time as she can
looking over the rail, seeing the future,
letting the splash wash away
everything that was Ekaterinoslav—
the dirt streets, the slash of trenches,
the wind blowing across open ground—
everything excepting the name.

Manifests

*"Note that Libau – now Liepāja was a town
in western Latvia, on the Baltic Sea."*
—From my cousin Martin Weiss who found the manifests

How big was the *S.S. Dwinsk*, out of Libau?
A ship of immigrants or a ship of fools,
for who but fools would cross that black sea
at the beginning of a late spring in the Russias?
They would have had only a few wooden planks
between themselves and a brutal death
that beat its barrel chest constantly against the boards,
a water beast trying to get at them.
Better, some would say, to stay home
where Cossacks only ransack every few years,
where the old tsar sits, too worried about his son's illness
to reach out his long arm against the Jews.
Some in Ekaterinoslav *did* stay, in familiar houses,
to die under the Cossack knives, the Nazi boot,
the deadly air of Chernobyl.

But we fools sailed on, crossing the sea,
where the horizon is sewn with a thin blue thread.
How big was the *Dwinsk*? Big enough to carry
the dreams of a single family into a future
where we become journalists, teachers, novelists,
lawyers, doctors, musicians, nurses, artists.
Where we own companies, run board meetings,
sell insurance, own stores, meet presidents and dictators.
Who needs streets of gold when we have this dream
beating against the ship's keel,
beneath the breastbone, manifested destiny.

Form 500 A
Department of Commerce and Labor
IMMIGRATION SERVICE

LIST OR MANIFEST OF ALIEN PASSENGERS FOR THE UNITED

Required by the regulations of the Secretary of Commerce and Labor of the United States, under Act of Congress approved February 20, 1907, to be delivered

S. S. „DWINSK".　　　　sailing from **Libau**　　　　　24. MRS 1914 , 19

No. on List	NAME IN FULL. Family Name.	Given Name.	Age. Yrs.	Mos.	Sex.	Married or Single.	Calling or Occupation.	Able to— Read.	Write.	Nationality. (Country of which citizen or subject.)	Race or People.	Last Permanent Residence. Country.	City or Town.	The name and complete address of nearest relative or friend in country whence alien came.	Final Destination. State.	City or Town.
1	Imoljanow	Timofey	27			m	cosmili	yes	yes	Russia	Russian	Russia	Bordginigi	wife Aljana Smoljanow Anazbizi Barina gour	N.Y.	New York
2	Jolin	Schimae	53			m	merchant	yes	yes	Russia		Russia				
3	Jolin	Clara-Alex	46			f	wife	yes	yes	Russia		Russia				
4	Jolin	Samuil	11				child	yes	yes	Russia		Russia		brother		
5	Jolin	Rachil	9				child	yes	yes	Russia	Hebrew	Russia	Eraterinoslaw	B Jolin Eraterinoslaw gour gor	Con	New Haven
6	Jolin	Wolf	7				child			Russia		Russia				
7	Jolin	Aron	4				child	no	no	Russia		Russia				
8	Rowinnaja	Zislia	30			f				Russia	Hebrew	Russia	Eripol	father L Rowinaya Eripol gour Felama	N.Y.	New York
9	Zelb	Josif	28			m	clerk	yes	yes	Russia	Hebrew	Russia	Odessa	brother J Zelbger Odessa gour Eleanos	N.Y.	New York
10	Segal	Mordxo	38			m				Russia	Hebrew	Russia		father Berice Segal Nowograd	N.Y.	New York
11	Rubinstein	Dawid	34			m	laborer	yes	yes	Russia	Hebrew	Russia	Sodiczew	brother J Rubinstein	N.Y.	New York
12	Tenenburg	Ocher	17			f	clerc	yes	yes	Russia	Hebrew	Russia	Kreschin	mother R Tenenburg	N.Y.	New York
13	Iwaszenno	Afron	23			m	farm laborer	yes	yes	Russia	Russian	Russia	Jenihonoy	wife M Iwaszenno Zeiew gour	Con	
14	Rudy	Michael								Russia						
15	Rudy	Karp	30			m	laborer	yes	yes	Russia		Russia		father Kalenin Rudy	Con	Waterburg
16	Rudy	Parascewa	25			f	housewife	yes	yes	Russia	Russian	Russia	Janischoni	Janischoni Kiew gour	Con	Waterburg
17	Rudy	Petr	2				child	no	no	Russia		Russia			Con	Waterburg
18																
19																
20																
21																
22																
23																
24																
25																
26																
27																
28																
29																
30																

The family's fortunes are often remembered
though the passage itself is not:
we came across second class, not steerage,
as if some sort of Jewish peerage had been conferred.
We'd money enough, coins not paper,
six hundred and sixty three dollars declared,
enough to make the voyage breathing real air
instead of the mould of rotting boards.
Not that we got to America any sooner than the poor,
but lorded over them, for they lay below us,
as we hoped they would in an America
where streets of gold instead of cobbles awaited,
where gefilte fish came in glass jars,
where matzah could be bought in packages,
and even the pirates—like Jean Lefitte—were Jewish.

Liberty Enlightening the World:
A Prose Poem

She is not yet thirty years old when the family first sees her,
yet she looks middle-aged, all those bronze draperies, and
the face of the sculptor's mother. A sudden burst of sun and
the patina glows, as if Miss Liberty stands in an aura. Rose
thinks the statue has smiled, but it is *she* who is smiling.

Once Lou finds them, swimming together in a sea of immigrants,
he tells them how Miss Liberty came from Europe in pieces.
Like our family, Will thinks. He has a fondness for metaphor,
for comparisons, for making things fit even when they do not.
Harry has found a pencil somewhere and has sketched the
statue with her lamp, her crown, though she looks rather like
a humped old lady with his mother's round face, her
braids twisted up to make Liberty's crown.

In the morning, they go by train to Connecticut, an Indian
name none of them can pronounce, though they all keep
trying. Only Rose turns to wave goodbye to the statue in the
harbor, though she does not get the direction quite right, her
palm pointing instead towards the Hudson River and its many
islands that look like scoops of ice cream in a rootbeer float.

As with all Yolen endeavors, it is the thought—the *gedank*
—that counts.

ELLIS ISLAND MATHEMATICS

The old world scrambles
for purchase in the new,
holding on with broken fingernails.

The cuticles of travel are raw,
bloody, chewed down, but still
we are safer here, or so we believe.

Here in the squawling ranks
of immigrants, the family is cattle
fearing the knacker's knife.

More feared, though, are the knives
of the horsemen of the steppes,
the unknown safer than the known.

The family tries on new names
as easily as a lady of means
tries a hat at the milliner's.

Lev becomes Louis, Lou.
Rachil Rose, Aron Harry.
My father, Wolf, tamed into Will.

Is it Yolin, Jolin, Yole? Manifest
transliterations change vowels,
consonants, till we all sound American,

Till we are all sound Americans,
only Jewish by extraction, attraction,
subtraction—Ellis Island mathematics.

I never met Grandpa Samson,
gone before my birth,
nor knew any of his dreams,
but his intentions are clear,
spelled out in a paper,
government issue no less,
for a man who never took issue
with any known government.
"It is my bona fide intention,"
the printed document declares,
though he only filled in the spaces,
renouncing all allegiances, fidelities,
whether he understood those words or not,
a scant four years after arriving in America.
Furthermore, he swore he was neither
an anarchist nor polygamist
and might have added,
"any old *ist* you *momzers* want,"
just to remain in the land of the free,
or at least in a land free of Cossacks.

So many days on water,
the white-topped waves wild,
Shumuel and Wolf stay by the rail
under Papa's unforgiving eye.
Shmuel will own his own boat one day,
be Captain Sam, a small tyrant
in the way of all captains.
In the second class cabin
that has become their home,
the others shrink from the relentless waves.
Mama and Rachil and Aron—
—never forget little Aron
who will become a world traveler
or Rachil who will live by the ocean
as if remembering the passage over.

So many hours in the red-brick building.
under the copper-domed towers
waiting to be accepted into America,
Papa holds tight to their papers
afraid they will be ripped from him,
sending the family back across the sea.
In a letter, Lou has warned him
of New World Cossacks in the Great Hall:
cadets, hustlers, con men
who would take their baggage tickets,
grab their children, steal their names.

So many hours under the barrel-vault ceiling,
in aisles outlined by iron railings,
Mama holds the children close,
keeping them from making friends
with lice-headed boys, coughing girls,
hundreds of them, thousands of them,
the ragged refuse coming to these shores.

At last, the inspector stamps their papers
ADMITTED.
Aron throws his little cap into the air.
"America!" Shmuel shouts. "Opportunity!"
a word he has just learned but does not understand.
Wolf just takes it all in, as he will later,
journalist, writer, storyteller.
The waiting over, Papa shepherds them
through a large green door,
with a sign in English he cannot yet read:
"*Push to New York*" but he pushes nonetheless.

They board the ferry, the double-decker
that spews them out into
that grotty, growling, growing city,
that gateway on the river, that paradisical door,
along with other newcomers, believers,
carrying old baskets filled with hope,
those greenhorns who still have years to go
before they are truly American,
before they are truly home.

GREENHORNS: 1914-1939

Lou's moustache, like inverted commas,
sets off his upper lip. Not a sneer, exactly,
but an attempted smile frozen in time,
as if he knows he's a looker, a ladies' man.
Two wives before he's barely grown
and still he's not tamed.
The others may be greenhorns, but Lou,
our first footprint in America, in fine boots, too,
marking his territory with those heels,
he's a considerable young man.
He's got cash and dash, the gold standard,
Check out the hat, the cane, the broad lapels.
He's no *nudnik* but knows stuff, this Dapper Dan,
bottler and bootlegger, ginger-haired gin miller,
lucky and legit mostly,
only his accent giving him away,
and the shadows that may be fear
in those tender, searching eyes.

MILLINERS

"A survey of workers in the 1900s in the US found that there were approximately 82,000 female milliners working at that time."
—WiseGeek

The girls have sewn before, of course;
in a shtetl one must do or do without.
Their careful threads have made
skirts, blouses, head scarves, underthings,
but nothing has prepared them for these tiny perfections,
invisible stitches, rows and rows of them.
They practice in their apprenticeships
till feathers gather themselves, brims roll effortlessly,
and needles—like those in the old tales of elves—
sew the expert seams.

This is no hobby, not a gift, but a respectable profession.
A girl who works hard can make a living,
sewing into the dusk of the New World,
till her fingers give out, her eyes.

Straw Bag

It sits on the floor of her bedroom,
a yellow straw bag bound by leather bands,
brass lock turned, key in her bedside table,
all packed for her trip home to the Ukraine.
She is not yet sure she can make a life here,
in the brangling American city, loud with many tongues.
Not here, without a cow, without chickens,
without neighbors she has known for half her life.
The bag is ready, bulging with clothes.
If she has to, she will sail away, without looking back,
though in all the years she has never gone
until it is finally too late to go.

MIDDLE CLASS

How quickly we thicken into the middle class,
a bit of fur here, a wide lapel there,
and suddenly we're walking these golden streets,
perfect advertisement for holy immigration.
Do not covet—that tenth rule from Sinai—
does not apply in this New World
where wealth falls like apples
straight down from bountiful trees,
where coveting means keeping up
with the Goldsteins, the Brombergs.
Hard work, hard work indeed,
but since when has a shtetl Jew
not known the iron hardness of work,
though rarely the sweet reward that comes after.

Great, great, great 932
grand parent.
Sampson & Minna
Yolen

BOTTLE

My grandfather was shiny as the bottles he sold,
what was on the outside as important as what sloshed within.
Kerosene in the old country warmed the family to life,
carted through the shtetl until we were rich enough
to come to America, second class.

In America, his horsepowered trucks,
carried bottles filled with Coca Cola,
long before the magic formula entered the mix,
a franchise sold too soon.
What was in the bottles served us then.
Later, it would have served us better.

On my shelf, a single seltzer bottle,
a memorial, a memory, a moment from the past,
when we had dreams, when we were almost rich,
who are now much richer
than grandfather ever dreamed of,
and somehow poorer as well.

They rarely played *durak* in Ekaterinoslav, too tired at night to set out the thirty-six cards. Here in New Haven, in the house with the six railroad apartments, it has become a cut-throat competition. No one wants to be last with cards in their hands, to end up the *durak*, the fool with epaulettes. "Like a Russian general," says Sylvia, "all medals and no mind." As they play, Caruso bellows from the gramophone, his voice a bit tinny, and they sing along loudly to *La donna e mobile* and *Over There*. At nine o'clock, an outside church bell rings the hours. Grandma makes the tea and puts out plates of *rugelah*, those sweet little bits of dough twisted around raisins, nuts, jam, and the apple fritters sprinkled with powdered sugar like snow-capped mountains. Weekends, the grandchildren are pulled from their beds, out from under the feather quilts, and given their choice of a pastry, which they stuff into their mouths quickly before Grandma changes her mind, before they are packed off back to bed.

GREENHORNS

1. An inexperienced or immature person, often easily deceived.
2. A newcomer unfamiliar with the ways of a place or group.
3. In New York City, late 19th, early 20th
century slang for a new immigrant.

When—the children ask—
will you try to learn English, Papa?
Stop reading Yiddish newspapers.
Stop counting coins as if they are rubles
instead of nickels and dimes.
When—Mama—will you stop making borscht?
It looks like blood. Smells like it, too.
And your kasha, pardon me for saying,
tastes like *nothing* warmed over.
How about a sausage, a burger, something fried?
We are here a year, two, three,
and still you swear in Russian, keep secrets in Yiddish,
only want us to keep company with other Jews.
We're no longer greenhorns.
Our schools are the melting pots America promised.
On the street, how good a boy is at stickball counts
more than the language he speaks at home.
In the factories we sit side by side
with Italians, Irish, gentiles from the Pale.
It's as if you didn't come to a new world,
but carried the old world here like tortoises,
such heavy shells on your backs.

COUSINS

Multiplying is easy if you start with eight.
If all the brothers and sisters save the youngest
have children, not singletons, but multiplicands,
the times table that will soon overwhelm
even the most welcoming of parents.
The logarithm of my cousins seems anarchic,
but love is the slide rule and the measure.
The oldest, years ahead of the youngest,
could be my parents, uncles, aunts.
In the photograph, they laugh out at me
though I was not yet born when that picture was taken.
As I write this, most are still alive,
careening along into their eighties and nineties,
but it is those faces captured in bright youth,
not yet maimed, shamed, tamed by life,
that call to me the most.
Family photos keep us young.

Yolen Family - Portchester N.Y. 1930

Top Jeanette, Bill, Aunt Rose
and Uncle Abe Dranoff, Bee, Eve Dranoff
and Rose Pinkus Yolen, grandma great great, lewis Pinkus
Sam's wife   Ruth grandma Yula Plotkin
                                 Gittle   Sylvia
Marshal   mother great quit Samson   Plotkin
Kressner   Vera grandma Yolen
           minnie
Micky minnie alvin elaine   Dorothy Yolen Eli
Plotkin Plotkin Kressner Dranoff   Mark Dranoff

Grandfather was determined to learn English
and speak as well as any American.
But those back-of-the-throat giveaways,
harsh gutturals, always marked him
incomer, immigrant, greenhorn.
Even four years later, papers in order,
he sounded foreign, not of this country
an embarrassment to his children.
Stories in English didn't come as easily
as they did tumbling out in Yiddish, Ukranian,
even Russian, but he told them anyway.
Nothing stops a Yolen from telling stories.
As for grandmother, a recipe works as well
in whatever language it is made,
though chopped liver is even better
in the old tongue.

BEYOND THE PALE: OCTOBER 1, 1933

Buried at Beth Midrash Hagadol cemetery in East Haven, CT.

Grandpa died here in New Haven,
well beyond the Pale,
a foot in two worlds,
and now a foot in the next.
We should have called him Tripod,
all those feet, but he was not a man
to have nicknames or make small talk,
though he could tell stories
with punch lines in Yiddish
so none of the grandchildren
could understand.

Is there understanding now,
some eighty years later,
as I, a grandmother myself
tell stories so nuanced,
the grandchildren cannot
be harmed or get the point?
We call it protection,
but who are we really protecting—
the new world or the old?

It begins with ending:
a funeral in New Haven.
Uncles with their
terrible cigars,
setting up a smoke screen
between themselves
and eternity.
Aunts in the kitchen,
kugels and knishes
popped out regularly
like little doughy babies.
Death is women's business,
like birth,
like life itself.

A tentative knock
interrupts the mourning.
A stranger at the door,
her eyes surprised by mascara,
stands shivering in the hall.
"I knew your mother, Manya, well."
So well, we think,
you did not know
we called her Mina, Minnie,
Minnie-ha-ha.
Never mind.
Grief makes us all courteous.
"Manya promised me
her fox fur," she says,
a claim so outrageous
it is honored.
She departs with the stole
around her thin neck,
the beady fox eyes
staring forward,
as if the fox always had its mind

set on travel.
It begins with endings:
a funeral in West Haven.
A man speaks wonderingly
of his dead wife
whom he has known
since childhood,
whom he has never really known.
Her dresser had been filled
with seventeen fox stoles,
hundreds of newspaper clippings.
Obituaries.
Notices of funerals
of absolute strangers.
Death obsessed her.
In the end, it possessed her.

A family story.
We tell it at every wake.
shivering outside death's door,
begging that bit of fox fur
to warm us into life.

The past will not lie buried.
Little bones and teeth
harrowed from grave's soil,
tell different tales.
My father's bank box told me,
in a paper signed by his own hand,
the name quite clearly: William.
All the years he denied it,
that name, that place of birth,
that compound near Kiev,
and I so eager for the variants
with which he lived his life.
In the middle of my listening,
death,
that old interrupter,
with the unkindness of all coroners,
revealed his third name to me.
Not William, not Will, but Wolf.
Wolf.
And so at last I know that story,
my old wolf, white against the Russian Snows,
the cracking of his bones,
the stretching sinews,
the coarse hair growing boldly
on the belly, below the eye.
Why grandfather, my children cry,
what great teeth you have,
before he devours them
as he devoured me,
all of me, bones and blood,
all of my life.

Velvul, Wolf, Will,
that child in Ekaterinoslav,
that boy holding the toy dog,
who said he knew no second tongue
but when dying babbled in Russian to me,
that young man who told a lie
about the place of his birth,
that father who taught me
songs, words, tales,
but little of love
or history,
or poetry.
That one.

I have written these
poems as resurrection.
I have molded these words
to reinvent moment and memory.
I have crafted these short lines
for the ones who come after,
my children's children.
For them I've created,
recreated really,
a lifetime,
a country,
a shtetl,
a home.

I can do no more.

A Small Glossary:

Bobbemysehs: Old wives' tales, fairy stories.

Borscht: beet soup, a classic Russian and Jewish dish.

Broche: A blessing.

Dank: Thanks.

Farfl: a noodle dish, small pellet noodles mixed with egg and matzoah for Passover.

Gedank: a thought.

Gefilte fish: Finely chopped whitefish mixed with crumbs, eggs, and seasonings, cooked in a broth, then made into balls and served chilled.

G-d: how very religious Jews write the name of God, which is not to be spoken aloud.

Greenhorn: Used in the late nineteenth and early twentieth century (especially in cities such as New York) for newcomers, immigrants, mostly derisively.

Kaddish: the Hebrew prayer for the dead.

Kasha: buckwheat groats.

Kugel: A Jewish baked pudding, usually of noodles and eggs, but often potatoes instead of noodles.

Knish: A piece of dough stuffed with potato, meat, or cheese that is either baked or fried.

L'chaim: A Hebrew toast. "To life."

Mitzvah: A good deed.

Momzer: Yiddish for *bastard.*

Nudnik: a bore, a pest, someone who wants something from you.

Pogrom: An organized, usually officially encouraged massacre of a minority group, most often the Jews of a region such as in Odessa, Russia.

Shul: Yiddish word for synagogue or temple.

Shtetl: a Jewish village, often within a larger Christian city or region.

Yenta: an old, gossiping woman.

Yiddish: a variant of medieval German which the Jews spoke in their shtetls and the ghetto folk used as a *lingua franca* in whatever country they dwelt.

Jane Yolen, often called "the Hans Christian Andersen of America," is the author of over 300 books, including *Owl Moon*, *The Devil's Arithmetic*, and *How Do Dinosaurs Say Goodnight*. The books range from rhymed picture books and baby board books, through middle grade fiction, poetry collections, nonfiction, and up to novels and story collections for young adults and adults. Her adult poetry has been published in literary journals, anthologies, and magazines.

Dr. Yolen's books and stories have won an assortment of awards—two Nebulas, a World Fantasy Award, a Caldecott, the Golden Kite Award, three Mythopoetic awards, two Christopher Medals, a nomination for the National Book Award, and the Jewish Book Award, among others. She is also the winner (for body of work) of the Kerlan Award, the 2012 de Grummond Medal, the World Fantasy Association Lifetime Achievement Award, Grand Master of the Science Fiction Poetry Association, and the Catholic Library's Regina Medal. Six colleges and universities have given her honorary doctorates. If you need to know more about her, visit her website at:

WWW.JANEYOLEN.COM